God said, "Let the water under the sky be gathered to one place, and let dry ground appear." And it was so. God called the dry ground "land," and the gathered waters he called "seas." And God saw that it was good.

—Genesis 1:9–10, NIV

To my parents, Carrol and Sharolyn,
who taught me about
God's ocean of love.
—Tina

God's Little Oceanographer

WRITTEN BY Tina Cho

ILLUSTRATED BY Marta Álvarez Miguéns

WATERBROOK

Little oceanographer,
let's take a trip to the sea.
Down, down, down under the waves
lies an **amazing world** to explore.

The sea is his, for he made it,
and his hands formed the dry land.
—Psalm 95:5, NIV

Out the window,
you will see
the **wonders** God has made.

When God created Earth,
He covered most of it with water.
The oceans surround the land.
Can you name them?
The **Atlantic**, **Pacific**, **Arctic**,
Indian, and **Southern**.

I was there when he set the limits of the seas,
  so they would not spread beyond their boundaries.
                                        —Proverbs 8:29

ATLANTIC
OCEAN

PACIFIC
OCEAN

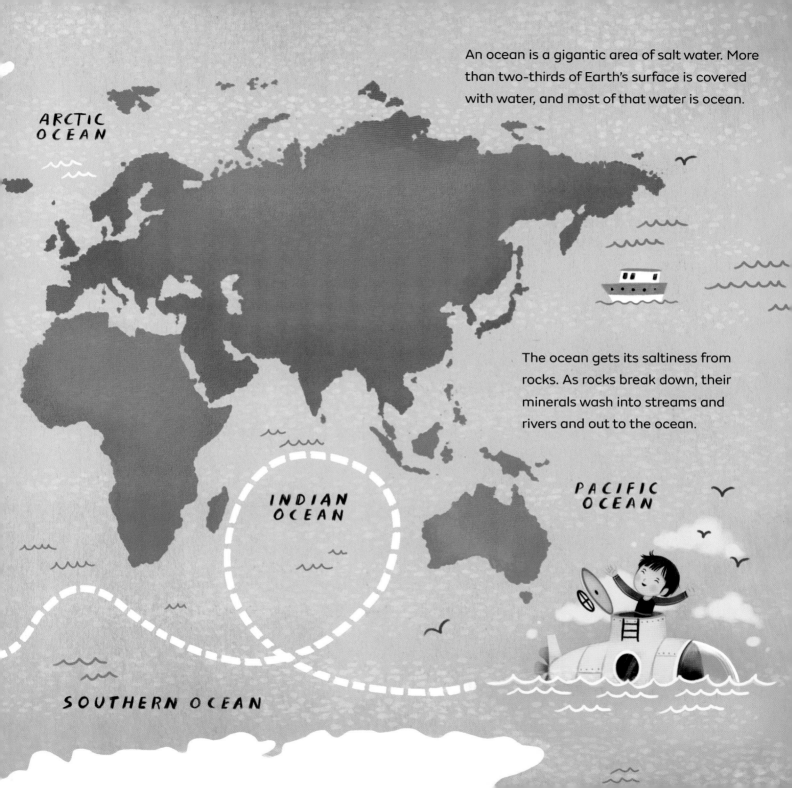

ARCTIC
OCEAN

An ocean is a gigantic area of salt water. More than two-thirds of Earth's surface is covered with water, and most of that water is ocean.

The ocean gets its saltiness from rocks. As rocks break down, their minerals wash into streams and rivers and out to the ocean.

INDIAN
OCEAN

PACIFIC
OCEAN

SOUTHERN OCEAN

Do you feel the ocean moving?
Wind blows across the surface,
making waves.
Cold water sinks,
and **warm water rises.**
Up and down,
back and forth,
the ocean **swirls around** the globe.
God put these paths into the sea,
just as **He creates paths** for your life.

Water moving from one place to another is called a current. Currents are caused by wind, tides, and the temperatures and salt content in the ocean. Gravity from the moon and sun pulls the water, creating low and high tides. The ocean is always on the move!

Seek his will in all you do,
and he will show you which path to take.
—Proverbs 3:6

Seaweed sways. Otters munch.
Dolphins jump. Sharks hunt.
Sailfish speed. Jellyfish drift.
An ocean buffet!
Every creature worships the Lord.
Join in the praise!

Great white sharks smile
with up to 300 teeth in
several rows.

Here is the ocean, vast and wide,
teeming with life of every kind,
both large and small.
—Psalm 104:25

Each dolphin has its own unique whistle, just as you have your own voice.

Otters float on their backs in forests of kelp, munching on sea urchins, mussels, and crabs.

The sunlight zone is the top layer of the ocean. It is 200 meters (660 feet) deep. Most of the ocean's animals live in the sunlight zone because of its warmth.

Jellyfish drift on the ocean currents, eating fish, crabs, shrimp, and plants.

Sailfish swim 70 miles per hour (113 kilometers per hour), making them the fastest fish.

Seaweed is a kind of algae. Seaweed can be red, green, or brown.

Look at the colorful **coral reef!**
Thousands of animals play hide-and-seek.
Sea turtles swim.
Seahorses bob.
Sea cucumbers feast.
Stingrays flap their fins to fly.
All were created by a **fun-loving** God!

Seahorses use their tails to hold
on to seagrass, camouflaging
themselves as they wait for food.

Coral polyps are animals that have their skeletons on the outside. As polyps multiply, their skeletons harden and form reefs. The largest coral reef is the Great Barrier Reef off the coast of Australia. Thousands of animals live in coral reefs.

Sea turtles eat seagrass and seaweed in the warm, shallow water around the reefs.

On the sandy seafloor, spotted eagle rays use their snouts to dig up clams and marine worms.

Sea cucumbers' poop makes the reefs healthier.

Let heaven and earth praise Him,
The seas and everything that moves in them.
—Psalm 69:34, AMP

In the dim twilight zone,
there are no plants here!
Whale sharks dive. **Squid** squirt.
Penguins fish. **Elephant seals** dine.
Anglerfish and **lantern fish** glow.
God's brilliance **shines** through every species.

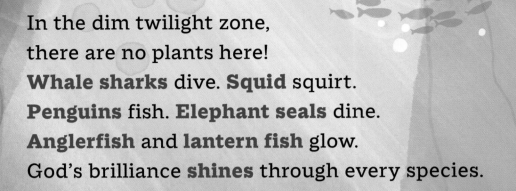

Strawberry squid sparkle
with lights and gaze out of
two differently placed eyes
to see prey above and below.

Elephant seals hold their breath for
up to two hours to hunt for octopuses,
squid, and eels.

The twilight zone is 200 to 1,000 meters (660 to 3,300 feet) deep. Animals that live or dive here for food have to brave the water pressure. Some animals are bioluminescent, making their own light to find food or scare away predators.

Whale sharks, the largest fish in the ocean, feed in the sunlight zone but dive into the twilight zone.

Each of the more than 245 species of lantern fish has a unique flashing signal made by the lights on their sides.

Female anglerfish have a lightbulb-like hook coming out of their forehead. It glows because of the bioluminescent bacteria living inside it.

Emperor and king penguins leave the ice to go fishing in the twilight zone.

They have seen the works of the Lord,
And His wonders in the deep.
—Psalm 107:24, AMP

Deeper down, dark as midnight,
live creatures great and small.
Dragonfish chomp.
Sperm whales click.
Black swallowers swallow.
Dumbo octopuses flap.
God sees these creatures,
just as **He sees you.**

Dumbo octopuses have earlike
fins and are the deepest-living
octopuses in the ocean.

Black swallower fish can swallow
fish bigger than themselves
because of their hanging stomach.

With an attractive light hanging
from their chin and sharp, pointy
teeth, female dragonfish don't
let a meal escape.

The midnight zone is 1,000 to 4,000 meters (3,300 to 13,100 feet) deep. Because there is no light from the surface, animals find food in other ways such as echolocation (bouncing sound waves off objects), bioluminescence (making their own light), and listening in the quiet deep.

Sperm whales use echolocation to find food such as squid, sharks, and fish.

Praise the LORD from the earth,
Sea monsters and all deeps.
—Psalm 148:7, AMP

On the pitch-black ocean floor,
a community of creatures
dwells by deep-sea vents.
Much of the ocean floor still needs to be explored.
God's creation **dazzles** in design.
What discoveries will you make?

Giant tube worms (which can grow more than six feet tall and look like tubes of lipstick) have no mouths, so bacteria in their bodies make food using poisonous gas from the sea vents.

Eyeless shrimp have eyes when young but lose their eyes as adults and grow a light-sensing organ on their backs.

He gives food to every living thing.
His faithful love endures forever.
—Psalm 136:25

The pitch-black seafloor and the water above it are known as the abyssal zone. It is 4,000 to 6,000 meters (13,100 to 19,700 feet) deep. Magma—melted rock inside Earth—pushes up through cracks in the ocean floor and creates underwater volcanoes. The seafloor doesn't just have volcanoes; you can also find canyons, mountains, and plains!

Blind, hairy white yeti crabs live near sea vents and feed on bacteria.

In the trenches in the seafloor
snailfish, cusk eels, and **amphipods** swim.
These critters have gooey or gel-like skin
and feed on "marine snow."
The God who **guides** creatures
in the deepest part of the sea
is near to you.
He will never leave you.

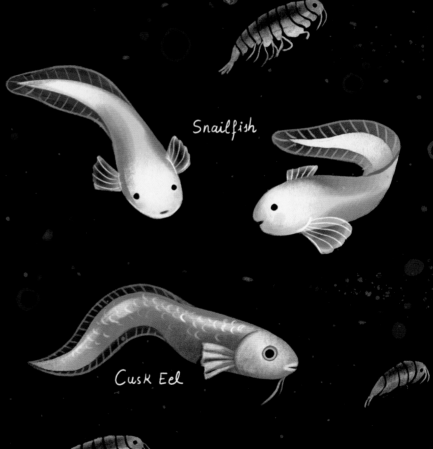

Snailfish

Amphipods

Cusk Eel

*If I ride the wings of the morning,
if I dwell by the farthest oceans,
even there your hand will guide me,
and your strength will support me.*
—Psalm 139:9–10

The trenches in the seafloor are called the hadal zone. The deepest spot on Earth is the Challenger Deep in the Mariana Trench. It is 11,000 meters (36,000 feet) deep. The hadal zone is still being explored as new technologies allow humans to safely discover all that God has made.

God made the ocean for you too!
It's full of **food to eat,**
gives you **air to breathe,**
supplies ingredients for **medicines,**
and sends just-right **temperatures** to where you live.
As big and powerful as the ocean may be,
He controls all of it.
What a mighty God!

Many people eat seafood like fish, crab, shrimp, and seaweed. Other foods like peanut butter, marshmallows, and ice cream have ingredients from seaweed. And of course, sea salt comes from the sea.

Phytoplankton

Although we live on land, humans rely on the ocean to provide oxygen, food, and other things we need. Tiny floating organisms called phytoplankton provide half the world's oxygen.

The ocean takes heat from the equator and sends it to the poles, setting weather patterns and controlling temperatures. The ocean is full of blessings for you!

Scientists use chemicals from sea creatures to create medicines, and ingredients from the sea are also used in toothpaste, shampoo, and skin-care products.

Mightier than the violent raging of the seas, mightier than the breakers on the shore— the LORD above is mightier than these!
—Psalm 93:4

Up, up, up above,
seabirds soar.
Puffins in the northern hemisphere,
albatrosses in the southern hemisphere,
terns and **gulls** all around,
fly and dive for tasty treats.

Puffins, sometimes called the clowns of the sea,
are powerful divers that live on islands and coastlines.

Many kinds of seagulls scavenge
the shorelines for food.

Roseate terns steal fish from other seabirds.

Wandering albatrosses have the largest wingspan of any flying bird in the world.

God created great sea creatures and every living thing that scurries and swarms in the water, and every sort of bird—each producing offspring of the same kind. And God saw that it was good.
—Genesis 1:21

You can have **fun** at the ocean—
swimming, fishing,
whale-watching, boating, bird-watching,
searching for sand crabs
and hidden creatures in tide pools.
The ocean **connects** you to God.
As you listen to the thundering waves,
think how our **powerful** God
shows His **goodness** to you.

People sail on cruises to exciting places.

Countries depend on the ocean to trade goods with other countries.

Many people spend time at the ocean, doing fun activities and enjoying wildlife.

The voice of the Lord is over the waters;
the God of glory thunders,
the Lord thunders over the mighty waters.
—Psalm 29:3, NIV

Little oceanographer,
you have a big **responsibility**
to care for the ocean God made
and all that lives within.
Your **helpful actions** can start
a ripple of kindness.

You gave them charge of everything you made,
putting all things under their authority.
—Psalm 8:6

Pollution harms the ocean and its creatures. Because of human activity, eight to ten million metric tons of plastic end up in the ocean each year. By 2050 there could be more plastic than fish in the ocean. An undersea explorer even found candy wrappers and a plastic bag in the Challenger Deep! We can protect the ocean and its creatures by using less plastic, recycling, and helping with cleanups.

Every **seashell, turtle hatchling, dolphin,** and **crab**
is a reminder of our great and creative God.
Yet *you* are His most **wonderful** and **special** creation.

Seashells once housed creatures such as snails, oysters, clams, and hermit crabs. Bright shells warned predators of a poisonous snack inside. Patterns on seashells camouflaged creatures in seaweed. Shiny insides of shells, known as mother-of-pearl, protected creatures from harmful invaders such as parasites.

*You made all the delicate, inner parts of my body
and knit me together in my mother's womb.*
—Psalm 139:13

The depths of the ocean
can't compare
with how deep
God's love is for you.

*Neither height nor depth, nor anything else in
all creation, will be able to separate us from
the love of God that is in Christ Jesus our Lord.*
—**Romans 8:39**, NIV

You are God's little oceanographer.

The earth will be filled with the knowledge of the
glory of the Lord as the waters cover the sea.
—Habakkuk 2:14, NIV

All Scripture quotations, unless otherwise indicated, are taken from the Holy Bible, New Living Translation, copyright © 1996, 2004, 2015 by Tyndale House Foundation. Used by permission of Tyndale House Publishers, Carol Stream, Illinois 60188. All rights reserved. Scripture quotations marked (AMP) are taken from the Amplified® Bible, copyright © 2015 by the Lockman Foundation. Used by permission. (www.lockman.org). Scripture quotations marked (NIV) are taken from the Holy Bible, New International Version®, NIV®. Copyright © 1973, 1978, 1984, 2011 by Biblica Inc.™ Used by permission of Zondervan. All rights reserved worldwide. (www.zondervan.com). The "NIV" and "New International Version" are trademarks registered in the United States Patent and Trademark Office by Biblica Inc.™

Text copyright © 2025 by Tina Cho
Cover art and interior illustrations copyright © 2025 by Marta Álvarez Miguéns

Published in the United States by WaterBrook, an imprint of Random House, a division of Penguin Random House LLC.

WATERBROOK and colophon are registered trademarks of Penguin Random House LLC.

ISBN 978-0-593-57943-5
Ebook ISBN 978-0-593-57944-2

The Library of Congress catalog record is available at https://lccn.loc.gov/2023028628.

Printed in China

waterbrookmultnomah.com

9 8 7 6 5 4 3 2 1

First Edition

Book and cover design by Ashley Tucker